What Can I...

See

Sue Barraclough

Raintree

Chicago, Illinois

© 2005 Raintree
Published by Raintree, a division of Reed Elsevier, Inc.
Chicago, Illinois
Customer Service 888-363-4266
Visit our website at www.raintreelibrary.com

Printed and bound by South China Printing Company.
09 08 07 06 05
10 9 8 7 6 5 4 3 2 1

Library of Congress Cataloging-in-Publication Data:
Barraclough, Sue.
  What can I see? / Sue Barraclough.
      p. cm. -- (What can I?)
  Includes index.
  ISBN 1-4109-2165-4 (library binding-hardcover) -- ISBN 1-4109-2171-9 (pbk.)
  1. Vision--Juvenile literature. I. Title: See?. II. Title. III. Series: Barraclough, Sue. What can I?
  QP475.7.B37 2005
  612.8'4--dc22

                                2004026302

Acknowledgments
The Publishers would like to thank the following for permission to reproduce photographs:
Alamy / Alan Copson City Pictures pp.**10-11**; Alamy / Imagestate p.**12**; Bryant-Mole Books p.**9** top; Collections p.**13**; Digital Stock p.**15** top; Getty Images / Imagebank pp.**20-21**; Getty Images / PhotoDisc pp.**14** inset, **15** bottom, **19** all images; Harcourt Education pp.**9** top (Chris Honeywell), **4-5**, **6**, **7**, **8**, **22-23** (Tudor Photography); Photolibrary p.**17** inset (OSF); PhotoVault pp.**14-15**; Powerstock pp.**16-17**; Powerstock / Brand X Pictures p.**18**.

Cover photograph reproduced with permission of Harcourt Education Ltd. / Tudor Photography.

Every effort has been made to contact copyright holders of any material reproduced in this book. Any omissions will be rectified in subsequent printings if notice is given to the publishers.

Some words are shown in bold, **like this**. You can find out what they mean by looking in the glossary on page 24.

Contents

Wake Up!

Eyes open! There's so much to see!

Rise and shine!

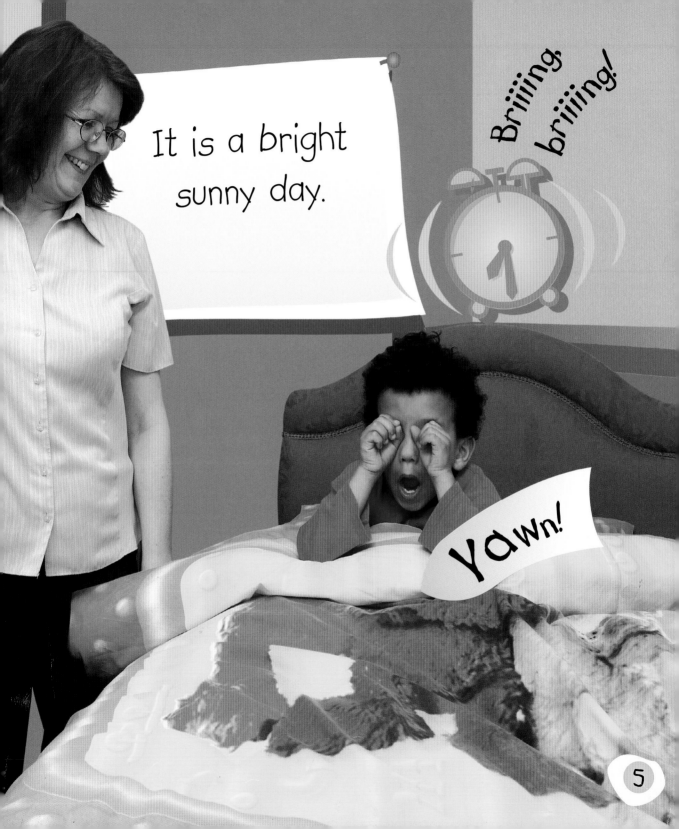

It is a bright sunny day.

Briiiing, briiiing!

Yawn!

5

Getting Dressed

Can you see the different colored t-shirts?

6

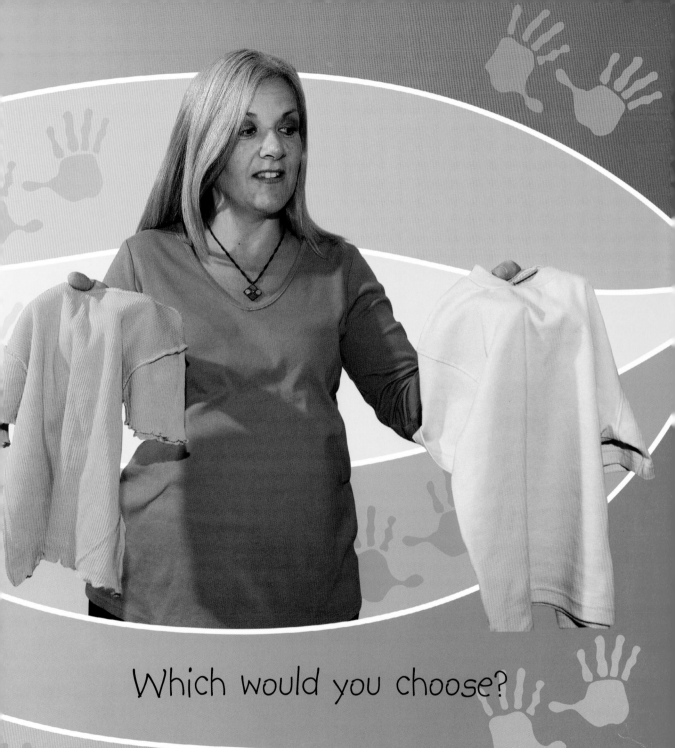

Which would you choose?

Going Out

Can you guess by looking at their toys?

At the Beach

What color is the sea?

Look at the beach. Can you see the colorful umbrellas?

Pails and Shovels

How many shovels do you see?

How many pails do you see?

Splish!

Splash!

Can you see what people are wearing
to protect them from the sun?

I spy...

These children are looking through a **telescope**.

14

What do the
children see?

17

A Sweet Treat

After playing, it's fun to
stop for ice cream.

Can you find the ice cream cone?

Yummy!

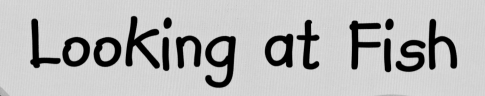

Looking at Fish

Do you see the bright, striped fish? How many do you see?

bubble

21

Night Sky

The moon and stars are bright in the sky. How many stars can you count?

What a **busy** day! Goodnight!

Yawnnnnnn!

23

Glossary

busy   filled with many things
telescope   tool used for seeing things that are far away

Index

Notes for Adults

Books in the *What Can I...* series encourage children to use their senses to actively explore the world around them.

Additional Information

The eyes detect colours and patterns of light and send this information to the brain in the form of nerve signals. Sight is one of the most important senses because the eyes send a huge amount of different information to the brain.

Follow-up Activities

- As part of a counting lesson, ask children to count the number of things of various colors they see in the room. Ask them to name other things of a designated color that are not in the room.

- As part of an art activity, ask children to create collages of things they might see in different settings. For example, the farm, the city, the playground, the pet store.